UNSOLVED QUESTIONS ABOUT THE UNIVERSE

BY GOLRIZ GOLKAR

CAPSTONE PRESS
a capstone imprint

Published by Capstone Press, an imprint of Capstone
1710 Roe Crest Drive
North Mankato, Minnesota 56003
capstonepub.com

Library of Congress Cataloging-in-Publication Data is available on the Library of Congress website.

ISBN: 9781669002680 (hardcover)
ISBN: 9781669002635 (paperback)
ISBN: 9781669002642 (ebook PDF)

Summary: What's inside a black hole? What are the sounds we hear from the depths of space? How did the moon form? When it comes to the realm beyond our planet, there are a whole lot of questions we're still trying to answer. Get ready to explore the unknown and discover how scientists are working to solve the mysteries of our universe.

Editorial Credits
Editor: Christopher Harbo; Designer: Sarah Bennett; Media Researcher: Svetlana Zhurkin; Production Specialist: Katy LaVigne

Image Credits
Associated Press: 7; Dreamstime: Hannu Viitanen, 16 (inset); Event Horizon Telescope Collaboration: 21; Getty Images: Aaron Horowitz, 20, Dean Mouhtaropoulos, 14, 15, ttsz, 19; NASA: ESA/CSA/STScI, 11, ESA/Zachary Schutte and Amy Reines (XGI)/image processing by Alyssa Pagan (STScI), 23 (top), JSC, 18, P. Garnavich (Harvard-Smithsonian Center for Astrophysics) and the High-z Supernova Search Team, 9 (top); Shutterstock: Ann Stryzhekin, 16–17, atanasis (background), cover and throughout, chromatos, 13, cigdem, 6, Dr Project (background), cover and throughout, ESB Professional, 12, gan chaonan, cover (bottom right), HUT Design, cover (bottom left), IgorZh, 9 (bottom), janez volmajer, 17 (inset), Josef Szeles, 27, Jurik Peter, 22, Matt Tilghman, cover (bottom middle), Paulo Afonso, 28–29, Roman Lyubimski, 25, Stefano Guidi, 26, Triff, cover (top), udaix, 23 (bottom), Vadim Sadovski, 4, 8

TABLE OF CONTENTS

INTRODUCTION
Our Mysterious Universe.........................4

CHAPTER 1
What Makes Up Most of the Universe? 6

CHAPTER 2
What Are Dark Matter and Dark Energy?........10

CHAPTER 3
How Do Matter and Antimatter Exist Together? ...12

CHAPTER 4
How Did the Moon Form?.....................16

CHAPTER 5
What's Inside a Black Hole?....................20

CHAPTER 6
What Are the Sounds We Hear in Space?.........24

CHAPTER 7
Are We Alone in the Universe? 26

Glossary.................................30
Read More 31
Internet Sites 31
Index 32
About the Author 32

Words in **bold** are in the glossary.

OUR MYSTERIOUS UNIVERSE

Earth is our home. Like the other seven planets in the solar system, it **orbits** the sun. The solar system is part of something even bigger. It is called a **galaxy**. It includes energy from stars. It also includes **matter** such as planets, moons, comets, and asteroids. And billions of galaxies exist beyond our own. Together, they make up the biggest system of all—the universe.

But here is a surprising fact: All of the known planets, stars, and other space objects make up only five percent of the entire universe. The rest is unknown. It cannot be seen directly. The universe is full of mysteries just waiting to be solved.

THE SCIENTIFIC METHOD

Scientists use a process called the scientific method to answer unsolved questions about the universe. They follow these steps:

- Ask a question
- Gather information
- Make a prediction
- Design an experiment to test the question
- Collect data
- Analyze data
- Draw conclusions
- Communicate results

CHAPTER 1

WHAT MAKES UP MOST OF THE UNIVERSE?

If only five percent of the universe is visible, what makes up the rest? Scientists noticed that **gravity** gives distant galaxies a distorted look. Gravity is an invisible force. It pulls objects toward each other. It keeps the planets in orbit around the sun. Based on how the galaxies looked, scientists wondered if there was some invisible matter in the universe pulling on them.

| The sun's invisible gravitational pull is powerful. It keeps all eight planets in our solar system in their orbits.

In 1933, an astronomer named Fritz Zwicky decided to investigate. He studied individual galaxies within a big cluster. He measured their speeds and brightness. He figured out the total mass, or amount of matter, in the cluster.

| Fritz Zwicky didn't just study the universe. He also developed jet engines and rockets that would one day help us reach for the stars.

FACT The universe formed about 13.8 billion years ago. Scientists know this by measuring the ages of the oldest stars and the rate of the universe's expansion.

The Hubble Space Telescope has been helping scientists unravel the secrets of the universe since 1990.

Zwicky made an important discovery. He found that a galaxy cluster has at least 10 times more invisible than visible matter. Invisible matter works like glue. It keeps galaxies together. Since it does not reflect or absorb light, it cannot be seen. Zwicky called this dark matter.

In 1997, the Hubble Space Telescope took pictures of dying stars called supernovas. They were exploding far off in the universe. Scientists realized that the universe is expanding rapidly. This was strange. If the universe is only made of visible objects, it should not be expanding. There must be invisible energy making this happen. Scientists named it dark energy.

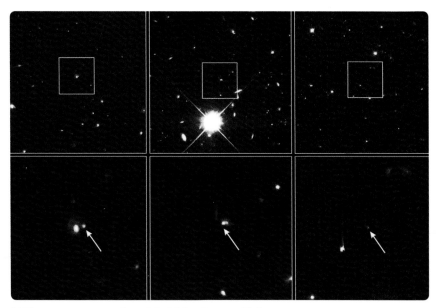

| The arrows in this Hubble Space Telescope image pinpoint three separate supernovas that exploded billions of years ago.

THE BIG BANG

The universe used to be very hot and tightly packed. Suddenly, all of its energy and matter began to expand and cool very quickly. Scientists call this event the Big Bang. Tiny **particles** of matter called **atoms** were formed. Atoms grouped together to create stars, planets, and other objects in space. The universe is still expanding today.

CHAPTER 2

WHAT ARE DARK MATTER AND DARK ENERGY?

Scientists believe dark matter and dark energy make up the other 95 percent of the universe. About 27 percent is dark matter. The other 68 percent is dark energy. However, scientists still do not know what either one is made of. Some think that dark matter contains unknown particles. Dark energy might come from these particles crashing against each other.

Scientists study dark matter and dark energy to understand how the universe is changing in size and shape. They want to know if the universe will keep expanding or stop at some point. Scientists study dark matter in different ways. They use sensors that detect heat particle movement. These particles show that dark matter is present. Scientists study dark energy by observing the energy waves in the universe left behind from the Big Bang. This helps them measure how fast the universe is expanding.

| Webb's First Deep Field image, taken by the James Webb Space Telescope, reveals thousands of galaxies in a tiny patch of sky about the size of a grain of sand held at arm's length.

CHAPTER 3

HOW DO MATTER AND ANTIMATTER EXIST TOGETHER?

The universe has a lot of matter. It makes up the stars in our galaxy, the planet we live on, and even our bodies. All of this matter is made of atoms that contain even smaller particles. They are called **protons**, **neutrons**, and **electrons**.

| Our galaxy, the closest part of which looks like a misty band of light in the clear night sky, is called the Milky Way.

MATTER ATOM

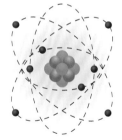

+ ● proton
○ ● neutron
− ● electron

ANTIMATTER ATOM

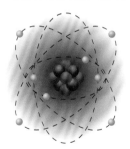

− ● antiproton
○ ● antineutron
+ ● positron

In addition to matter, the universe also has a small amount of **antimatter**. Antimatter is just like matter, except it has the opposite electric charge. This is the amount of electricity matter holds. For example, an electron has a negative charge. Its antimatter "partner" has the same mass but a positive charge. Because of their opposite charges, matter and antimatter destroy each other when they meet.

When the universe was born, only light energy existed. As it expanded, equal amounts of matter and antimatter were made. They should have canceled each other out. Yet something stopped this from happening. Even stranger, more matter than antimatter remained.

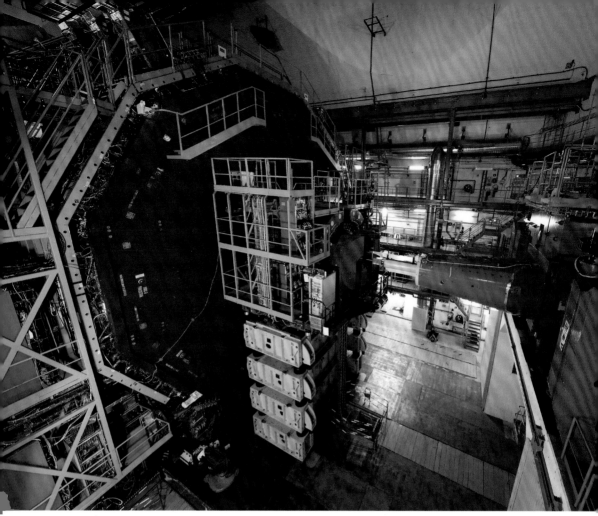

| Massive, high-tech machines are used to make and study antimatter at CERN, the world's largest particle physics laboratory, located in Switzerland.

Life exists today because there is more matter than antimatter in the universe. If an equal or greater amount of antimatter existed instead, all matter would be destroyed. There would be no living things at all.

FACT Antimatter is used in some medical equipment, such as scanners that help detect cancer.

| Scientists study data on a large bank of computer screens in a control room at CERN.

Some scientists think that the Big Bang created more matter than antimatter. Others believe that some particles changed from antimatter to matter. Today, scientists continue to study antimatter. They have built powerful machines that detect and examine antimatter particles. They are even learning how antimatter may be useful.

CHAPTER 4

HOW DID THE MOON FORM?

Hundreds of moons orbit the planets in our solar system. Mars has two moons. Jupiter has 79. Saturn has 82! And as you know from looking up at the night sky, Earth has one moon. Astronauts have even visited our moon, but scientists don't know how it came to be.

| Mars and its moons, Phobos and Deimos

All moons likely formed from dust and gases. They swirled around the planets when the solar system was created. Scientists once believed that Earth used gravity to capture the moon as it passed by. Others suggested that Earth and the moon were created together. Maybe the moon was a piece of Earth that had broken off.

| Jupiter and one of its moons, Io

Scientists continue to study the moon today. Between 1969 and 1972, astronauts collected rock and soil samples from the moon's surface. These samples show that Earth and the moon are made from similar materials.

| Lunar sample 61016 is also known as Big Muley. The 25.8-pound (11.7-kilogram) rock is the largest sample astronauts brought back from the moon.

FACT Mercury and Venus are the only planets in our solar system that have no moons.

THE MOON'S FORMATION

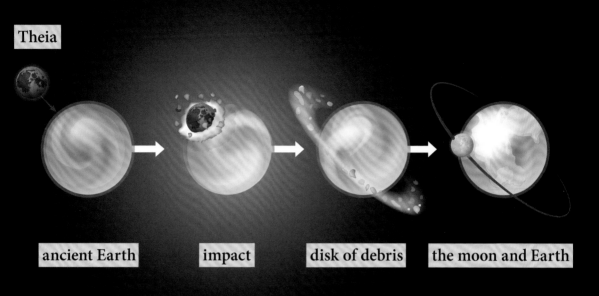

Theia

ancient Earth | impact | disk of debris | the moon and Earth

| A small planet's impact with Earth may have created the debris that would eventually bind together to form the moon.

Scientists now have a new theory. They think that the moon formed after a giant impact. A long time ago, a small planet called Theia likely collided with Earth. The **debris** from the impact collected in an orbit around Earth. Over time, the moon was formed from the debris. Scientists hope that future space missions will give more answers about Earth's closest neighbor.

CHAPTER 5

WHAT'S INSIDE A BLACK HOLE?

Black holes are one of the universe's biggest mysteries. A black hole is a part of space where matter has collapsed upon itself. The matter is densely packed into a tiny point. The gravity of a black hole is very strong. Nothing, including light, can escape it. A black hole has an imaginary boundary near its center. It is called an event horizon.

| Black holes are invisible, but we know they exist because of the way light and matter behave around them.

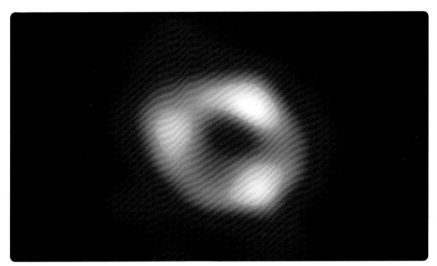

| In 2022, scientists revealed the very first image of the supermassive black hole at the center of our galaxy, surrounded by a ring of light.

Stellar black holes form when stars explode and collapse. They are found in all galaxies. Supermassive black holes form when galaxies are created. They can contain more mass than several billion suns. They are thought to lie at the center of most galaxies. Our own Milky Way galaxy has one.

Black holes can't even be seen with telescopes. Scientists know they exist by observing their effect on matter. They look for objects in space that are being pulled by strong gravity and stars that seem to orbit nothing at all. In both cases, black holes are likely nearby.

Scientists use scientific laws to understand black holes. They believe that if a star or spacecraft were to get too close to a black hole, it would be pulled toward the event horizon. It would stretch and flatten out. This is called spaghettification. The object would look like spaghetti! Its mass would be squished into the black hole. Escape would be impossible.

Scientists are learning about black holes every day. Telescopes photograph black holes tearing up and swallowing stars. Recent photographs have even shown a black hole in another galaxy releasing gas that forms new stars. Until now, scientists never knew that black holes could help create new stars. How this is possible remains a mystery.

| Nothing, not even a star or its light, can escape the powerful gravitational pull of a black hole.

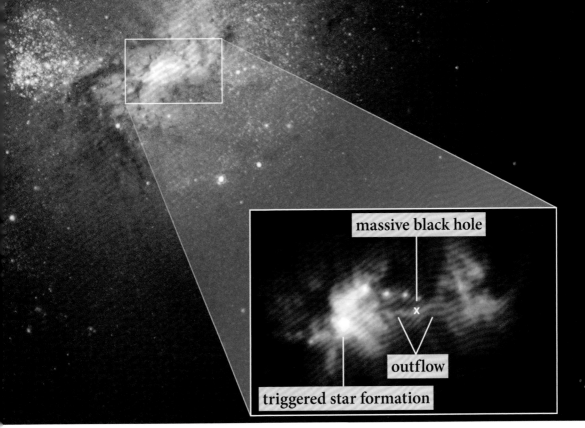

massive black hole

x

outflow

triggered star formation

| A black hole in a dwarf starburst galaxy is causing new stars to form.

wormhole

INSIDE A BLACK HOLE

A black hole is extremely powerful. Its intense gravity even changes scientific laws about space-time. Near a black hole, time actually slows down. Some scientists think that the bottom of a black hole could be a tunnel called a wormhole. It would lead to another point in space and time, such as a different galaxy.

CHAPTER 6

WHAT ARE THE SOUNDS WE HEAR IN SPACE?

Space is a quiet place. This is because space has no air. On Earth, sound waves travel through the vibration of atoms in air to reach our ears. In the vacuum of space, there are no atoms to travel through. Yet scientists can hear a roaring sound in the universe. How is this possible? And what is causing it?

Scientists use instruments to detect other kinds of waves that can travel through space. These include light, gravitational, magnetic, and radio waves. Through a process called sonification, they change these waves into sound waves humans can hear.

FACT Astronauts can't hear any pounding or drilling they do while on space walks. The only sounds they can hear are the pumps and fans inside their spacesuits and their crew mates' voices in their helmet radios.

| Scientists use radio telescopes to scan the universe for radio
waves coming from the depths of space.

Scientists can listen to the hum of a black hole.
But they can't find the source of the space roar. Some
believe it may be leftover energy from star formation.
Stars give off heat in the form of radio waves that can
be detected by instruments. It could be the sound
of gases swirling around. One thing is certain—the
universe is noisy.

ARE WE ALONE IN THE UNIVERSE?

If the universe is so enormous, does life exist outside Earth? Scientists are still unsure. It is very hard to find evidence of **extraterrestrial** life. Some people claim to see unidentified flying objects, or UFOs. Mysterious patterns called crop circles have been found in fields. Still, there is no definite proof of beings visiting us from other worlds.

| Some people believe crop circles, such as this one in an Italian wheat field, are the work of beings from other worlds.

| While the search for life on other planets continues, we can only imagine how alien worlds might be different from our own.

Many scientists think there must be other **habitable** planets in the universe. Water and oxygen make life possible. For now, Earth is the only known planet with liquid water on its surface. Scientists use telescopes in space to look for habitable planets. They think there may be as many as 300 million habitable planets in the universe. However, none have proven to have life yet.

| The SETI Institute's Allen Telescope Array is a group of 42 radio telescopes used to detect radio signals coming from deep space.

Scientists at the SETI Institute in California look for signs of extraterrestrial life. One way they do this is by using radio telescopes on Earth to listen for sounds from space. These telescopes have detected mysterious radio signals. Some scientists believe the signals are coming from passing comets. Others think they could be messages from alien life.

The universe is still an unknown place. It is made up of billions and billions of galaxies. And each of those galaxies is packed with countless stars, planets, moons, and wonders beyond imagination. But science makes it possible to learn more about the universe every day. And one day, technology and human curiosity may just solve its greatest mysteries.

GLOSSARY

antimatter (AN-ti-mat-ur)—matter that is made up of antiparticles

atom (AT-uhm)—the smallest particle of an element

debris (duh-BREE)—the scattered pieces of something that has been broken or destroyed

electron (uh-LEK-trahn)—a tiny particle in an atom that travels around the nucleus

extraterrestrial (ek-struh-tuh-RESS-tree-uhl)—coming from or existing outside the Earth or its atmosphere

galaxy (GAL-uhk-see)—a cluster of millions of stars bound together by gravity

gravity (GRAV-uh-tee)—a force that pulls objects with mass together

habitable (HAB-uh-tuh-buhl)—safe, comfortable, and clean enough to live in

matter (MAT-ur)—particles of which everything in the universe is made

neutron (NOO-trahn)—one of the very small parts in an atom's nucleus

orbit (OR-bit)—to travel around an object in space

particle (PAR-tuh-kuhl)—a small piece of matter

proton (PRO-tahn)—a positively charged particle in the nucleus of an atom

READ MORE

Barr, Catherine. *The Universe and its Mysteries.* New York: Rosen Publishing, 2022.

Nargi, Lela. *Mysteries of the Universe.* North Mankato, MN: Capstone, 2021.

Regan, Lisa. *Our Solar System.* New York: Rosen Publishing, 2021.

INTERNET SITES

European Space Agency: The Universe
esa.int/kids/en/learn/Our_Universe/Story_of_the_Universe/The_Universe

NASA Science: Space Place
spaceplace.nasa.gov

National Geographic Kids: Passport to Space
kids.nationalgeographic.com/space

INDEX

antimatter, 13–15
astronauts, 16, 18, 24
atoms, 9, 12, 13, 24

Big Bang, 9, 10, 15
black holes, 20–23, 25

dark energy, 8, 10
dark matter, 8, 10

extraterrestrial life, 26–28

galaxies, 4, 6, 7, 8, 11, 12, 21, 22, 23, 29
gravity, 6, 17, 20, 21, 22, 23

matter, 4, 6, 7, 8, 9, 10, 12–15, 20, 21
moons, 4, 16–19, 29

planets, 4, 5, 6, 9, 12, 16, 17, 18, 19, 27, 29

radio waves, 24, 25, 28

scientific method, 5
solar system, 4, 6, 16, 17, 18
sounds, 24–25, 28
stars, 4, 5, 7, 8, 9, 12, 21, 22, 23, 25, 29

telescopes, 8, 9, 11, 21, 22, 25, 27, 28

wormholes, 23

ABOUT THE AUTHOR

Golriz Golkar is the author of more than 60 nonfiction and fiction books for children. Inspired by her work as an elementary school teacher, she loves to write the kinds of books that students are excited to read. Golriz holds a B.A. in American literature and culture from UCLA and an Ed.M. in language and literacy from the Harvard Graduate School of Education. Golriz lives in France with her husband and daughter.